Incredible Inventions

POEMS SELECTED BY
Lee Bennett Hopkins

ILLUSTRATIONS BY
Julia Sarcone-Roach

Greenwillow Books
An Imprint of HarperCollins Publishers

Fig. 9.

Fig. 4.

Fig 10.

To
Charles J. Egita
who is *always* inventive . . .
　　　　　—L. B. H.

To my parents, for their love and support
　　　　　—J. S. R.

Incredible Inventions
Text copyright © 2009 by Lee Bennett Hopkins
Illustrations copyright © 2009 by Julia Sarcone-Roach
All rights reserved. Manufactured in China.
Page 32 constitutes an extension of the copyright page.
www.harpercollinschildrens.com

Acrylic and mixed media were used to prepare the full-color art.
The text type is Insignia.

Library of Congress Cataloging-in-Publication Data

Hopkins, Lee Bennett.
Incredible inventions / selected by Lee Bennett Hopkins ;
illustrated by Julia Sarcone-Roach.
p. cm.
"Greenwillow Books."
ISBN: 978-0-06-087245-8 (trade bdg.)
ISBN: 978-0-06-087246-5 (lib. bdg.)
1. Inventions—Juvenile literature.
I. Sarcone-Roach, Julia. II. Title.
T48.H737 2009
600—dc22   2008003830

First Edition 10 9 8 7 6 5 4 3 2 1

Greenwillow Books

TASTE TINGLING
TONGUE TEMPTING
TONSIL ENTICING
TOE TAPPING
TOOTH TICKLING

 ORANGE

FUN SHAPES?

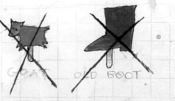

PINE
DANGEROUS?
STAR
BUNNY
GOAT
OLD BOOT

Contents

TUNA

SAUSAGE

CHEESE

BANANA
STRAWBERRY
JELLY
SPRING
LIME
ORANGE
BEAN CHEESE
MANGO
BLUE
RABBIT
LEMON
PINEAPPLE
FIG

PRUNE?

A
B
C
D

A
B
C
D
E

F

APPLICATION FILED OCT. 4, 1923

Two Puzzling

Amy Ludwig VanDerwater

If two people purchase puzzles
printed perfectly the same
one will treat it as a job
one will play it like a game.
One will line up edges neatly.
One will sort it out completely
all alone or with a friend
flipping, fitting end to end.
One will quit for quite a while.
One will work without a sound.
One will drop the box of pieces
spending days at lost and found.
From outside in to inside out
one will giggle. One will pout.

But on that final finish day

"Got it!"

"Got it!"

each will say.

One will pull it back apart
one will place it in a frame
if two people purchase puzzles
printed perfectly the same.

Ode to Blue Jeans

Rebecca Kai Dotlich

See them strolling
in their jeans
from subway ads
to magazines.

Rock 'n' rollers.
Construction crews.
Everybody
loves their blues.

Faded, torn,
shabby, new,
with cowboy boot
or tennis shoe,

ranchers, writers,
racers, teens,
the world's in love
in love . . .
          with JEANS.

Roller Coaster

Joan Bransfield Graham

slow   c l i m b

            fast

            drop

stomach still

       at the top

curves

               d   s

                i   p

          backflips

pull SCREAMS

      from your lips

heart-in-throat

       wind-in-hair

raise-your-hands

       if you DARE

          look back

where you've been

              catch your breath . . .

         ride

             again!

The Straw——1888

Drew Lamm

A simple sipping instrument

s
p
r
u
n
g

f
r
o
m

Marvin Stone's

i
m
a
g
i
n
a
t
i
o
n.

Paper strips wound round his pencil,
glued together—*poof*! A new invention.
Eventually sealed with wax, preventing leaks,
swilling spirals leading lemonade to puckered lips.

Castle building, dreaming, pure play
one person wondering on any old day.

What
might
you

i
n
v
e
n
t
t
o
d
a
y
?

Basketball Seasons

John Sullivan

I
trees in flower
an air ball rolls
into greening grass

II
sweltering night
one player left on the court
alone with stars

III
chill gusts
the thump of a bank shot
over crackling leaves

IV
ice-glazed rim
young shooter nails a three-pointer
with a snowball

The Tale of Fig Newton

Sandra Gilbert Brüg

Charles M. Roser
an Ohio baker
    back in 1891:
    a mover, a shaker
    a fine cookie maker—
whipped up a cookie
with cake and fig jam.

James Henry Mitchell
a fellow cake baker—
    sensing potential
    enticed by a dream
soon proudly invented . . .
a cookie machine!

A simple machine
sporting two fitted funnels
    one placed inside
    of the other, just so—
one for the jam
one for the dough.

By cranking a lever
there oozed out, most willing
    a thick figgy filling
    a smooth fruity taste—
wrapped up in a blanket
of *heavenly* cake.

The cookie was charming!
Completely disarming
    a tiny bit chewy
    delightfully sweet.
"The Newton," so named—
ballooned into fame.

One hundred years later . . .
we love them today!
    I wonder what
    Roser and Mitchell
    would say?

The Ferris Wheel

Elizabeth Upton

What kind of mind
dreamed of flying more than
two thousand people
around and around on a great wheel
two hundred sixty-four feet into the air?

A mind that fused two bridge arches
into one steel wheel,
stunning as the Eiffel Tower,
moving with the grace of a
blue whale plunging into deep sea.

Riders lifted
rocking gently,
sailing through the air on a sky schooner—
seeing far things from a soaring height
transported by Ferris's physics of delight.

Take the Escalator

Kristine O'Connell George

Take the escalator,
    no need to climb the stairs—
    use the people freighter.
    But please don't linger there,
    step forward now, step on—
    choose your personal stair.
    (All yours, no need to share.)

Hold tight the rubber rail,
    and take a ride to where
    the moving staircase goes.
    Remember: Watch your bags,
    your fingers, and your toes.

Watch now, you're almost there,
    don't daydream, be aware,
    because when you reach your floor,
    your stair will slide away,
    like a closing dresser drawer.

Now! Step off. No, not later—
    Escalator's a terrible waiter.

Brushes Rule

Constance Andrea Keremes

Time was when fingers did the trick,
Pat this, part that, do it quick.

But hair's no simple thing today,
You have to gel, highlight, spray.

You need a brush to get things right.
(A comb will only tug and bite.)

The problem is, which brush to use?
There are a million ones to choose.

The penny pocket model's fine
For simply keeping things in line.

But whirly spikes and curls call for
A brush that does a whole lot more.

Short tips, long tips? Flat brush or round?
The possibilities astound.

If you want to go deluxe,
Beware—you'll have to pay big bucks.

Confused and want to shave your head?
Relax—and ponder this instead.

Plain or fancy; plastic, wood,
A brush will keep you looking good.

Inside the Box

Ann Whitford Paul

Inside the crayon box
long pointed fingers
decked out in paper wraps
joust for attention.

    "Choose me!"
    "No, me!"
    "I'm the right color for seeds."

But who says a seed
must be brown?
  A field of corn green?
  A flat tire black?
As you take crayons
from their box,
break out of your own box.

Turn your paper
into a whole new world.

What to Do with a Popsicle

Lee Bennett Hopkins

Lick
   and
lick
   and
lick
   and
lick

until
nothing
is
left
but
the

P o p s i c l e   s t i c k

Band-Aid

J. Patrick Lewis

Rosebud of blood
   Bubbles and smears.
I brush the mud
   And dry my tears.

Thankful I have
   That peace of tape
From Mom or Dad
   For cut and scrape.

Out of the blue
   A first-aid kit
Turned "Ouch" to "Oooh"
   And in a bit

This three-inch patch
   Will let me play
Because the scratch
   Is "stripped" away.

The Signal's Lament

Alice Schertle

Green, yellow, and red, going round in my head
Like the same old tedious tune.
I think you can see that it just isn't *me*—
I long for magenta, maroon.

Or aquamarine! Why couldn't *that* mean
It's time for the traffic to STOP?
Purple for SLOW, and to tell them to GO
A cadmium orange would pop.

Let's broaden the scope: Is it too much to hope
I could shine in cerulean blue?
Or how about taupe? They'd just have to cope
With an interesting color or two.

What a driver's surprise! It would open their eyes
If I flashed them a lavender glow,
Then changed to chartreuse, with a finish of puce—
It would get their attention, I know.

I may look like a pole, but I have the soul
Of an artist, a star, a flamingo!
And speaking of pink, that's a winner, I think,
Add a touch of vermilion and BINGO!

"In Here, Kitty, Kitty"

Marilyn Singer

Edward Lowe was not a loafer.
    Edward Lowe was not a quitter.
He saw a need, he worked with speed
    to bring the country Kitty Litter.

When his neighbor's cat tracked ashes
    on dainty paws, a-patter-pitter,
He suggested, he had tested
    absorbent clay for Kitty Litter.

He wasn't Edison or Whitney.
    Still feline owners didn't titter.
Oh, to think he banished stink
    with tons and tons of Kitty Litter!

Velcro

Maria Fleming

As fasteners go,
I'm unsurpassed.
My stickiness
will flabbergast.

I'm King of Cling,
my grip won't slip
until you choose
to rip the strip.

Buttons? Bah!
Buckles? *Please*.
Neither has
my strength, my ease.

I sneer at snaps,
the lowly lace.
They lack my lock,
my fierce embrace.

Just try to name
a greater gripper.

(Don't even *think*
of saying *zipper*.)

In New Running Shoes

Fran Haraway

I bet I could set a new record for running.
I'll race like a greyhound, astonishing, stunning
The ones left behind with a view of my back.
I bet I'd be way out in front of the pack.

I bet I could set a new record for leaping.
I'll rise like a lion. My feet will be keeping
Me steady as—quickly—I lengthen my stride.
I bet I'll be racing ahead of the pride.

I bet I could set a new record for climbing
I'll move like a monkey—sure-footed and timing
My climb so that when I'll be ready to stop,
I bet I will lead the whole troop to the top.

I'll run, leap, and climb—and I can't wait to see
The places these new shoes will soon carry me.

Behind the Inventions

Jigsaw Puzzles—1766

John Spilsbury, a London engraver and mapmaker, would be shocked to see the number of pieces that make up one of today's jigsaw puzzles. The count might be five hundred pieces, one thousand pieces, three thousand pieces, or more!

In 1766, Spilsbury created jigsaw puzzles by starting with maps adhered to flat hardwood. Using a fine-bladed saw, he cut the maps into several small pieces. His object was to help boys and girls learn geography in an interesting way.

Cardboard puzzles were introduced in the late 1800s. Today, jigsaw puzzles feature everything from replicas of great art to cartoon characters, holidays, and events from history and sports.

Blue Jeans—1873

Orphaned at sixteen, Levi Strauss trained as a tailor in Bavaria, Germany. In 1853, when he was in his mid-twenties, he settled in San Francisco, California. There he opened a dry goods store and sold supplies to gold-rush miners.

In 1872, one of his customers, the tailor Jacob W. Davis, told Strauss how he made durable work pants by placing metal rivets at the points of strain in pocket corners and at the base of the fly. Davis could not afford the eighty-one dollars needed to apply for a patent, so he suggested that Strauss pay for the paperwork to take out a patent together. On May 20, 1873, the patent was granted. Today blue jeans are worn all over the world. A pair of early Levi's is in the permanent collection at the Smithsonian Institution in Washington, D.C.

Roller Coaster—1884

John August Miller strived his entire life to get his roller coasters to go higher, steeper, faster, make sharper turns, even spin upside down.

Born August John Mueller in 1874, in Homewood, Illinois, he changed his name when he began working with LaMarcus Adna Thompson, a roller-coaster designer and engineer. Thompson is credited with having created the first roller coaster, which debuted in Coney Island, New York, in 1884. The following year he patented his "Roller Coasting Structure." Miller eventually became Thompson's chief engineer.

In 1920, Miller and Harry C. Baker created a joint company, Miller and Baker, Inc., which gave Miller the impetus to create a large number of coasters. Three years later he established his own company, where he perfected, manufactured, and invented many of the technologies for roller coasters as we know them today.

His devotion to coasters never ceased. He died on June 24, 1941, while working on a coaster in Houston, Texas.

Drinking Straws—1888

As you sip a soft drink or lemonade through a straw, you can thank Marvin Stone. On January 3, 1888, Stone patented a "spiral winding process" that led to the manufacturing of the first paper drinking straws.

Stone designed the straw to be eight-and-a-half inches long, with a diameter just wide enough to stop things such as seeds from getting stuck in the tube. Prior to Stone's paper straws, beverage drinkers used natural rye grass or reed straws.

1766

1873

1884

1888

Basketball—1891

We don't usually think about a game being invented, but basketball was!

In 1891, as a student at the YMCA Training School in Springfield, Massachusetts, Canadian-born James Naismith was given an assignment to create a diversion that would keep fellow students interested in exercising indoors during a brutal New England winter. He came up with the concept for "Basket-Ball" and the game's original thirteen rules.

The first match was played with a soccer ball and two peach baskets used as goals. Hoops and nets were introduced two years later.

In 1936, Naismith saw the game introduced in the Olympics, held in Berlin, Germany. The Naismith Memorial Basketball Hall of Fame opened on February 17, 1968, in Springfield. It's been relocated twice since then, and on September 28, 2002, its permanent Springfield home was opened to the public.

Today, more than 450 million people in 212 countries have hoop dreams.

Fig Newton Cookies—1891

Fig Newtons, soft, chewy cookies filled with fig jam, have been nibbled for more than one hundred years.

Charles Martin Roser, a cookie maker from Ohio, created the recipe and sold it to the Kennedy Biscuit Works (now Nabisco), in Newton, Massachusetts, in 1891. That year, James Henry Mitchell invented a machine that worked like a funnel within a funnel. One funnel supplied jam, the other pumped out dough, and together they made the first mass-produced Fig Newton cookies.

More than one billion Fig Newtons are devoured each year.

Ferris Wheel—1893

We can thank bridge builder George Washington Gale Ferris, Jr., born in Galesburg, Illinois, for the thrill of a ride on a Ferris wheel.

The first Ferris wheel began operating on June 21, 1893, at the Chicago World's Fair. It was 264 feet tall, about the height of a twenty-six-story building, and had thirty-six wooden cars that could each hold forty people sitting or sixty people standing, plus a conductor. The cars were twenty-seven feet long, thirteen feet wide, and nine feet tall. More than two thousand people could ride at one time. The ride, costing fifty cents, netted a whopping $726,000 during the fair.

Today, smaller versions of the Ferris wheel are among the most popular rides at theme parks, fairs, and carnivals all over the world.

Escalator—1891–1900

Jesse Wilford Reno and Charles Seeberger are both credited with the invention of the escalator. Reno invented a "moving stairway" or "inclined elevator" in 1891, and first exhibited it as an amusement ride in Coney Island, New York, in 1895. Within several months, more than 75,000 people went on the ride that lifted them seven feet above the ground.

Seeberger redesigned the device in 1897 and named it by combining the word "elevator" with *scala*, the Latin name for steps.

By 1900, improved versions of the escalator were installed in department stores, exhibition halls, and railway stations.

1891

1891

1893

1891–1900

Hairbrush—1898

Although brushes were used millions of years ago for cave paintings, it took a long time before they were applied to hair grooming. Throughout the centuries people experimented with creating the perfect hairbrush.

Quite possibly, the hairbrush you use today is the type invented by Lyda Newman, an African American from New York City. On November 18, 1898, Newman acquired a patent for a new, improved brush with synthetic bristles that provided ventilation by having recessed air chambers. The brush was easy to keep clean, and quite durable. Today, hairbrushes range in cost from several dollars to hundreds of dollars.

Crayola Crayons—1903

What a colorful history two cousins created!

Edward Binney and C. Harold Smith, owners of a paint company in New York City, produced a number of modern-day products, including slate pencils and dustless chalk to be used in schools. In an effort to create better-quality, affordable wax crayons to be used by children, they combined paraffin wax with pigments to produce crayons as we know them today. In 1903, they marketed a box containing eight colors and sold it for a nickel. Their crayons became an overnight success. Binney's wife, Alice, formed the word "Crayola" by combining two words—the French word *craie*, meaning chalk, and *oleaginous*, oily.

In 1988, Crayola crayons were added to the permanent collection at the Smithsonian Institution in Washington, D.C. On February 6, 1996, the one hundred billionth crayon rolled off the production line at Binney & Smith headquarters in Easton, Pennsylvania. Today, more than 120 different colors are produced.

Popsicles—1905

One night in 1905, eleven-year-old Frank Epperson filled a glass of soda powder with water and left it outside his San Francisco home with a wooden stirring stick in it. Fortunately temperatures dropped below the freezing point of 32 degrees Fahrenheit. Waking up the next morning, Frank found his mixture frozen, with the stick protruding up like a handle. He named his newfound invention the Ep-sicle.

It took another eighteen years for Frank to apply for a patent. Several factors worked against him: Rarely did temperatures drop below freezing in San Francisco, and the home freezer had not yet been invented. Married with five children and in debt, he decided to forge ahead with his idea. He found a six-inch glass tube to be a perfect mold and invented a machine to manufacture the frozen treat and another machine to stamp his name on the wooden stick.

In 1925, he sold his invention to the Joe Lowe Company, which later became part of Good Humor-Breyers. More than one billion Popsicles are consumed each year in the United States alone. Orange has always been the favorite flavor.

Band-Aid—1920

During Josephine Dickson's first week of marriage in 1917, she cut herself twice with a kitchen knife while preparing dinner. More cuts, scrapes, and burns followed.

Luckily, her husband, Earle, worked for Johnson & Johnson, a company that manufactured gauze and adhesive tape. After several weeks of witnessing Josephine's accidents, Earle began to prepare ready-made bandages by placing squares of cotton gauze on adhesive strips.

A year later the first adhesive bandages were produced and sold as Band-Aids. Eventually Earle was made vice president of the company.

1898   1903   1905   1920

Traffic Signal—1923

The entire world is a safer place because of Garrett Augustus Morgan, an African-American inventor.

Although other inventors experimented with developing traffic signals, Morgan was the first to acquire a United States patent for the electric traffic signal.

Morgan, the son of former slaves, was in his fifties when the automobile became popular. In 1922, he saw a car hit a horse and carriage, leaving the driver unconscious and the horse gravely injured. He immediately began working on a way to direct traffic automatically. His invention, a "visible indicator," was patented on November 20, 1923. He sold the rights to the General Electric Company for forty thousand dollars. Modern traffic lights are based on Morgan's original concept.

In addition to the traffic signal, he also invented another life-saving wonder—the gas mask.

Kitty Litter—1947

Edward Lowe gave the world something to "meow" about.

After serving in the United States Navy from 1941 to 1945, Lowe went to work at his father's company in Cassopolis, Michigan. The company sold industrial absorbents such as sawdust, sand, and clay. In 1947, a neighbor asked him for some sand to replace the ashes she used in her cat's litter box. He suggested absorbent clay instead. The neighbor was thrilled that her cat no longer tracked ashes from its sooty paws all over the house.

Lowe packaged the clay in five-pound bags and tried to sell them for sixty-five cents. No one bought them, so he gave them away. Once cat owners had used the product, they asked for more and were willing to pay for it.

In 1985, he founded the Edward Lowe Foundation, headquartered in Cassopolis, Michigan, which is designed to encourage American entrepreneurs.

Velcro—1955

Getting caught in a sticky situation was rewarding for George de Mestral, an inventor born in a small village near Lausanne, Switzerland.

One summer day in 1948, he took his dog for a nature hike. They both returned covered with burrs, prickly seed cases that cling to clothing and animal fur. Curious about the burrs, he used his microscope to observe how their small hooks clung to the tiny loops in the fabric of his pants.

De Mestral patented Velcro, a hook-and-loop way to fasten fabrics and other materials, in 1955. The name Velcro stems from a combination of two French words, *velour* (velvet) and *crochet* (hooks).

Modern Athletic Shoes—1964

Modern athletic shoes were invented by two men: Philip Hampson ("Buck") Knight, a twenty-year-old runner on a track team at the University of Oregon, and his coach, Bill Bowerman. Tired of clumsy running shoes, the duo formed a company in 1964 to market a lighter, more durable, and more comfortable shoe designed by Bowerman. Bowerman's technical breakthrough was the invention of the first lightweight shoe, created using latex, glue, and his wife's kitchen waffle iron.

Little did they know what success would lie ahead. In 1972, their company became Nike, named for the Greek goddess of victory. Today, Nike has become one of the leading sports companies in the world.

1923   1947   1955   1964

Acknowledgments

For works in this collection, thanks are due to:

Curtis Brown, Ltd. for "Ode to Blue Jeans" by Rebecca Kai Dotlich, copyright © 2009 by Rebecca Kai Dotlich and "What to Do with a Popsicle" by Lee Bennett Hopkins, copyright © 2009 by Lee Bennett Hopkins. Both reprinted by permission of Curtis Brown, Ltd.

Sandra Gilbert Brüg for "The Tale of Fig Newton." Used by permission of the author, who controls all rights.

Maria Fleming for "Velcro." Used by permission of the author, who controls all rights.

Kristine O'Connell George for "Take the Escalator." Used by permission of the author, who controls all rights.

Joan Bransfield Graham for "Roller Coaster." Used by permission of the author, who controls all rights.

Fran Haraway for "In New Running Shoes." Used by permission of the author, who controls all rights.

Constance Andrea Keremes for "Brushes Rule." Used by permission of the author, who controls all rights.

Drew Lamm for "The Straw—1888." Used by permission of the author, who controls all rights.

J. Patrick Lewis for "Band-Aid." Used by permission of the author, who controls all rights.

Ann Whitford Paul for "Inside the Box." Used by permission of the author, who controls all rights.

Alice Schertle for "The Signal's Lament." Used by permission of the author, who controls all rights.

Marilyn Singer for "'In Here, Kitty, Kitty.'" Used by permission of the author, who controls all rights.

John Sullivan for "Basketball Seasons." Used by permission of the author, who controls all rights.

Elizabeth Upton for "The Ferris Wheel." Used by permission of the author, who controls all rights.

Amy Ludwig VanDerwater for "Two Puzzling." Used by permission of the author, who controls all rights.

the
Birth of Velcro

A DRAMATIC RE-ENACTMENT